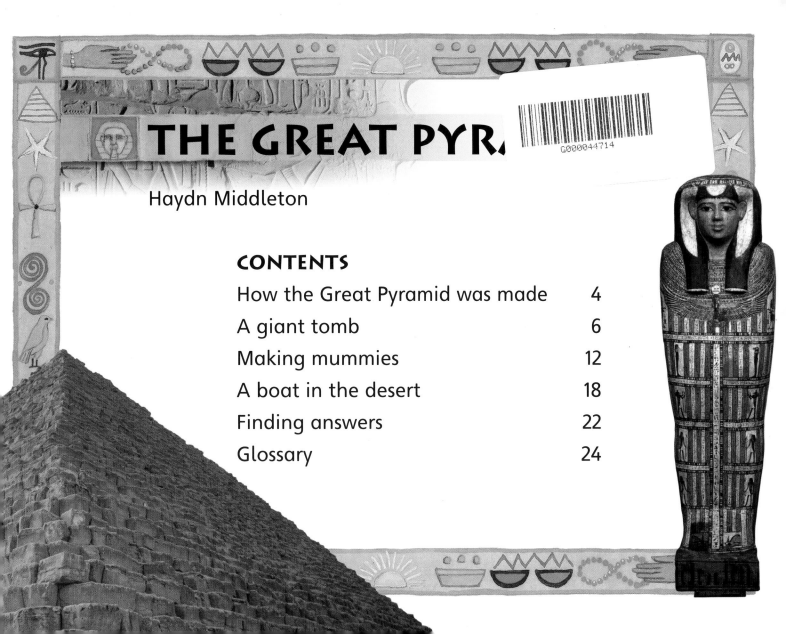

THE GREAT PYRA

Haydn Middleton

CONTENTS

How the Great Pyramid was made   4

A giant tomb   6

Making mummies   12

A boat in the desert   18

Finding answers   22

Glossary   24

The pyramids at Giza in **Egypt** are one of the world's most famous sights. Thousands of people visit Egypt every year to marvel at these awesome buildings, but not many people know how they were built, or why. This is the story of the biggest of Giza's pyramids – the Great Pyramid.

HOW THE GREAT PYRAMID WAS MADE

The Great Pyramid was built over 5 000 years ago. It is made from more than two million blocks of stone, making it the largest pyramid in the world. After the stone had been dug out of the ground and made into blocks, each block had to be put carefully in just the right place. The Great Pyramid took over 23 years to complete!

**The Great Pyramid is made of huge stone blocks.
It stands in the desert, near the River Nile.**

DID YOU KNOW?
For 4,000 years, the Great Pyramid at Giza was the tallest building in the world, reaching around 145 metres. That's 10 metres taller than the London Eye!

The stone blocks were very heavy and must have been difficult to lift. Today we use powerful **machines** to move heavy objects like stone, but the people of **Ancient** Egypt had less powerful tools.

Maybe the people of Ancient Egypt moved the blocks like this.

The workers who built the pyramids had to do much of the building by hand. **Archaeologists** (say 'arkee-ollo-jists') think that they dragged the blocks, then pushed and pulled them into the right place using ropes and ramps.

A GIANT TOMB

The Great Pyramid looks strange from the outside, but inside it is even stranger! A doorway in the side of the pyramid opens onto a long, dark tunnel leading to a little room. There is no one in this room now, but archaeologists believe that 5,000 years ago, the Egyptians left a dead body here. They think that the Great Pyramid is like a huge grave, called a **tomb**.

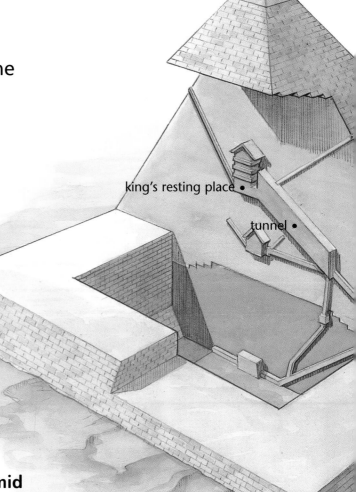

king's resting place •

tunnel •

Inside the Great Pyramid

Archaeologists believe that the Great Pyramid was the tomb of King Khufu (say 'koo-foo'). He was once the King of Egypt.

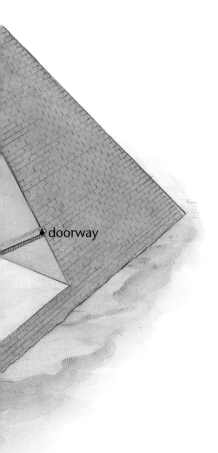

doorway

Archaeologists believe that King Khufu's body once rested here inside the Great Pyramid.

KING KHUFU

King Khufu lived in the 26th century BC and became king of Egypt when he was in his twenties. He got thousands of workers to start building his pyramid tomb right away! He wanted everyone to know how important he was, even after he died. That is why he wanted the Great Pyramid to be so huge.

This is a statue of King Khufu.

The people of Egypt wanted to say prayers to King Khufu after he died, so they built a **temple** in front of the Great Pyramid. Today most of the temple's stones are missing, but archaeologists can work out what the pyramid and temple once looked like.

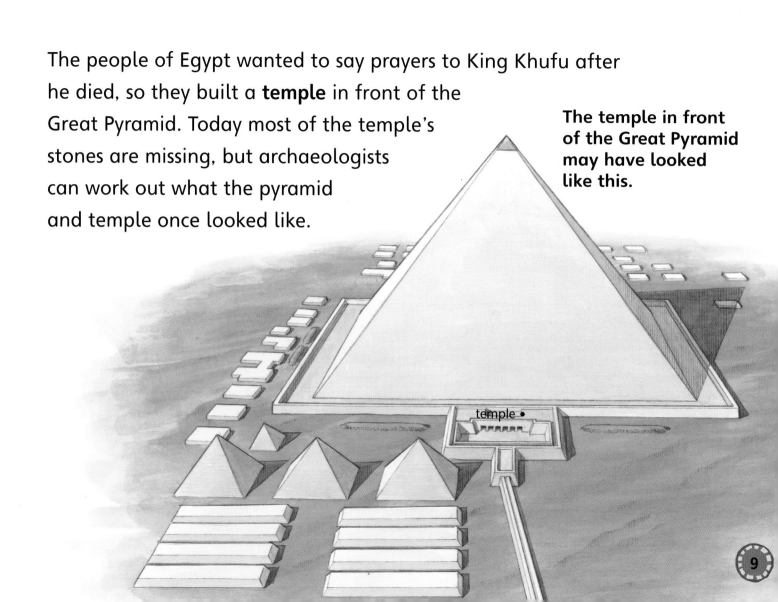

The temple in front of the Great Pyramid may have looked like this.

temple •

WRITING ON THE WALLS

King Khufu wanted people to remember his name after his death, so he had his name **inscribed** on a wall inside the Great Pyramid. That is how we know the Great Pyramid was built for him.

The writing looks strange to us. Today we use letters to write with, but the people of Ancient Egypt wrote with pictures. They used lots of different pictures called '**hieroglyphs**' (say 'hi-row-gliffs'). Some hieroglyphs represented whole words, and some represented a sound.

The Rosetta Stone

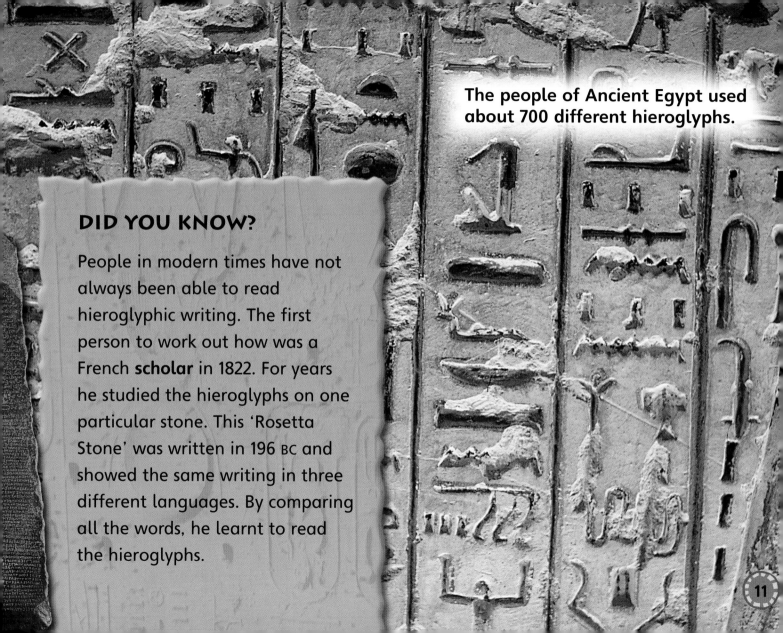

The people of Ancient Egypt used about 700 different hieroglyphs.

DID YOU KNOW?

People in modern times have not always been able to read hieroglyphic writing. The first person to work out how was a French **scholar** in 1822. For years he studied the hieroglyphs on one particular stone. This 'Rosetta Stone' was written in 196 BC and showed the same writing in three different languages. By comparing all the words, he learnt to read the hieroglyphs.

MAKING MUMMIES

Dead bodies rot and then turn to dust, but people in Ancient Egypt wanted King Khufu's body to last forever. To stop King Khufu's dead body from rotting, they first took out his insides. Then they made his body dry and wrapped it up in cloth. This **preserved** the body.

A body that is preserved like this is called a 'mummy'. The people of Ancient Egypt turned lots of bodies into mummies – even cats, snakes and crocodiles! We know this because some mummies have lasted until today. You can see them in museums.

The Egyptians used many special ingredients to dry out a dead body and make it into a mummy. In one pyramid it is written that 'seven **sacred** oils' were used. Archaeologists know that many of these came from plants. Beeswax was also an important ingredient.

This is an Ancient Egyptian drawing of the stages of making a mummy.

MUMMY HOUSES

King Khufu's people wanted to be buried near him. They thought this would make them look important after they died, so they made smaller tombs near the Great Pyramid. These tombs were like whole houses. There were even streets between the houses, too. It was like a little city for mummies!

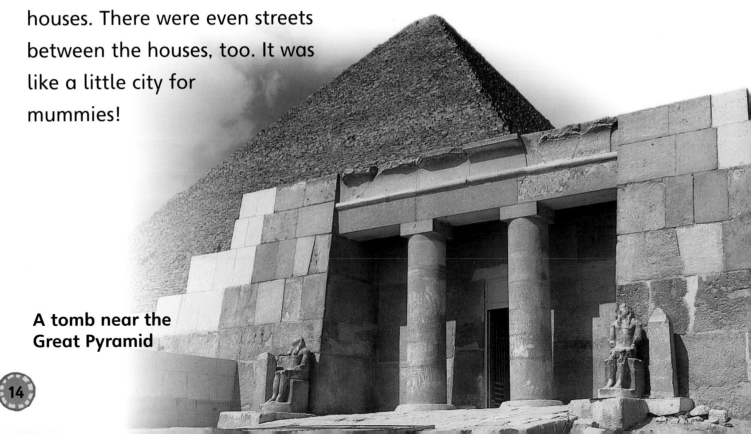

A tomb near the Great Pyramid

The tombs had two levels. The mummy was always put downstairs, and in an upstairs room there was a statue of the dead person. There were statues of the dead person's family too. Visitors to the tomb used these upstairs rooms. They left food and drink and presents behind to show they still cared for the dead person.

This statue of a dead person is in a tomb. He has his hands out for presents!

UNDER THE SUN

Archaeologists are not sure why the Great Pyramid was built where it is, but they can look at clues and try to work it out. They know that the sun was very important to the people of Ancient Egypt. The people thought that the sun was a god called Ra, and that Ra was King Khufu's father.

• Each day the sun rises in the east of the sky – this may be why the front of the Great Pyramid faces east.
• Each day the sun sets in the west – this may be why the Great Pyramid stands on the west bank of the great River Nile.

A BOAT IN THE DESERT

The people of Ancient Egypt left food and presents in the temple in front of the Great Pyramid because they thought King Khufu's mummy would need them in the **afterlife**. Food and presents were not the only things left for the dead king ...

In 1954, archaeologists discovered a big pit beside the Great Pyramid containing more than a thousand pieces of wood. They dug all the bits up and began to fit them together. It was like a giant jigsaw puzzle, and it took ten years to complete. When it was finished, all the bits made ... a boat! Why did the people of Ancient Egypt leave a boat for their dead king?

The boat that was found next to the Great Pyramid

Reaching Ra

Archaeologists think that the boat was linked to Ra, the sun god of Ancient Egypt.

The people of Ancient Egypt thought that Ra rowed across the sky in a boat. He began his trip in the east – that is where the sun rises every morning. He finished his trip in the west – that is where the sun sets every evening.

They thought that King Khufu was the son of sun god Ra, so the king's mummy would need a boat to reach Ra after he died.

The people of Ancient Egypt thought Ra crossed the sky in a boat.

FINDING ANSWERS

Many people visit the Great Pyramid at Giza every year. They want to learn more about King Khufu and Ancient Egypt, and to see the huge pyramid for themselves.

The Great Pyramid is still a bit of a mystery, and even archaeologists don't know everything about it. Why is it so big? Why is it that shape? Only the people of Ancient Egypt know all the answers, but they died thousands of years ago.

Maybe one day you will visit the Great Pyramid. Then you can come up with your own answers!

GLOSSARY

afterlife   life after death – in some religions it is believed that a person's life continues in some way after they have died

ancient   very old

archaeologist   a person who studies the past by looking at old buildings and objects

Egypt   a country in the north-eastern part of Africa

hieroglyphs   pictures used for writing, instead of letters

inscribe   to write or carve something into a surface

machine   a device that makes it easier to do hard work, such as lifting or moving something

preserved   specially treated to stop it from rotting

sacred   holy, or to do with religion

scholar   someone who studies a particular subject

temple   a religious building; somewhere people go to pray

tomb   a room or building used as a grave